Life Lessons from My Dog

Life Lessons from My Dog

Donna K. Maltese

INSPIRATION FOR DOG LOVERS

BARBOUR
PUBLISHING

Contents

Introduction

Welcome to *Life Lessons from My Dog*—a book just for dog lovers! Here you'll find all-new devotional readings celebrating faith, fun, and furry canines, as well as God's love, voice, security, strength, friendship—and more! In addition, there's a plethora of other dog-centric inspiration: scripture, prayers, quotes, and quips, sure to bring a smile to your face. Ideal for pooch enthusiasts of all ages, *Life Lessons* promises bountiful blessings. It's a perfect way to start or end a day, or to snatch a quick pick-me-up in between, all the while growing closer to God and experiencing His joy through the antics of our furry friends!

Taming the
Beast

No one can tame the tongue;
it is a restless evil and
full of deadly poison.

James 3:8 nasb

Although dogs, descendants of the gray wolf, were domesticated thousands of years ago, some still seem to have a wild side. Such was the case with Buck, the German-shepherd-mix beast we'd rescued from the pound.

Buck liked to bolt. If anyone held him (or the kitchen door) too loosely, nine times out of ten, he would break free and run for his life—usually down to the pizza parlor to pick up some fresh, just-delivered Italian rolls. One night he bolted, got struck by a car, and kept going. The next morning, my husband and I, thinking Buck had died from injuries received in the accident, broke the news about his early demise to our little girl. Ten minutes later we found Buck sitting on our porch, panting, hale and hearty, ready for his breakfast kibble.

Like Buck, the human tongue can sometimes run wild, leading us to say things we later regret. So before speaking, consider applying a "rein check" to your words, making sure they are encouraging, not hurtful. Or another option may be to simply muzzle your mouth by stuffing it with a nice, fresh Italian roll.

A dog's bark is as much a signature as its scent. Every bark is a full, clear statement of existence—"I bark, therefore I am." It is unrestrained, unedited, and unabashed.

JOHN O'HURLEY

Dogs do always bark at those they know not, and. . .it is their nature to accompany one another in those clamors.

SIR WALTER RALEIGH

He who barks last, barks best.

PAMELA McQUADE

Recollect that the Almighty, who gave the dog to be companion of our pleasures and our toils, hath invested him with a nature noble and incapable of deceit.

Sir Walter Scott

Although the dispositions of dogs are as various as their forms. . .to the credit of their name be it said, a dog never sullies his mouth with an untruth.

Alfred Elwes

The reason dogs have so many friends is because they wag their tails instead of their tongues.

Unknown

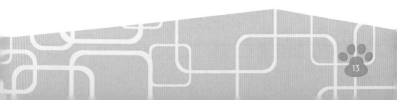

If I was sad, then he had grief, as well—
Seeking my hands with soft, insistent paw,
Searching my face with anxious eyes that saw
More than my halting, human speech could tell;
Eyes wide with wisdom, fine, compassionate—
Dear, loyal one, that knew not wrong nor hate.

MERIBAH ABBOTT

Dogs howl to "talk" to other members
of the pack. Generally speaking, a howl says
"Where are you?" If your dog howls
when left alone, it is bored.

BRUCE FOGLE

One dog barks at something,
the rest bark at him.

CHINESE PROVERB

The dog is the most faithful of animals
and would be much esteemed were it not
so common. Our Lord God has made His
greatest gift the commonest.

MARTIN LUTHER

So once again, I, the Lord All-Powerful, tell you, "See that justice is done and be kind and merciful to one another! Don't mistreat widows or orphans or foreigners or anyone who is poor, and stop making plans to hurt each other."

ZECHARIAH 7:9–10 CEV

"And you must love the Lord your God with all your heart, all your soul, and all your strength."

DEUTERONOMY 6:5 NLT

But the Holy Spirit produces this kind of fruit in our lives: love, joy, peace, patience, kindness, goodness, faithfulness, gentleness, and self-control. There is no law against these things!

GALATIANS 5:22–23 NLT

Though we don't look at all like them, dogs accept us as part of their pack. Our weaknesses—small, feeble ears and noses, two legs, and a distinct lack of fur—don't keep them from loving us.

PAMELA MCQUADE

I like a bit of a mongrel myself, whether it's a man or a dog. They're the best for everyday.

GEORGE BERNARD SHAW

I have a little brindle dog,
Seal-brown from tail to head.
His name I guess is Theodore,
But I just call him Ted. . . .

He plays around about the house,
As good as he can be,
He don't seem like a little dog,
He's just like folks to me.

MAXINE ANNA BUCK

Wagging the Tail

Nothing in all creation will ever be able to separate us from the love of God that is revealed in Christ Jesus our Lord.

ROMANS 8:39 NLT

I was having one of those days. It began with oversleeping, which made me late for an appointment. Later, while running errands, I backed my SUV into a brand-new red Mustang convertible in a parking lot. Once home, my mood worsened, and I found myself speaking harshly to a loved one. Disgusted with myself and the day's events, I headed up to my room. There was Durham, our latest rescue hound, napping on the bed. I threw myself on top of the quilt and began to cry. The next thing I knew, the tail-wagging Durham, overjoyed to see the miserable me, was licking my face. I looked directly into his eyes and saw nothing but love.

No matter how badly our day goes or how miserable we feel, our dogs will love us unconditionally. Such is the love of God. Nothing can separate us from His all-encompassing compassion for us. Even through our tears, we have a place in God's heart. That's something to wag our tails about!

Whoever loveth me, loveth my hound.

THOMAS MORE

It's nice to have a pet that offers unconditional love, someone who doesn't talk back. I love cats, but cats take you on their terms. My golden retriever could have a broken leg, and his teeth could be falling out, but if I walk in the door, he'll wag his tail until it hurts.

BOB VETERE

We long for an affection altogether ignorant of our faults. Heaven has accorded this to us in the uncritical canine attachment.

GEORGE ELIOT

Love is patient, love is kind. . . .it is not proud. . . . it is not self-seeking, it is not easily angered, it keeps no record of wrongs. It always protects, always trusts, always hopes, always perseveres.

1 Corinthians 13:4–5, 7 niv

This is real love—not that we loved God, but that he loved us and sent his Son as a sacrifice to take away our sins.

1 John 4:10 nlt

Always remember to forget
the things that made you sad.
But never forget to remember
the things that made you glad.
Always remember to forget
the friends that proved untrue.
But never forget to remember
those who have stuck by you.

IRISH BLESSING

The motion of [a dog's tail] is full of
meaning. There is the slow wag of anger;
the gentle wag of contentment; the brisker
wag of joy: and what can be more mutely
expressive than the limp states of sorrow,
humility, and fear?

ALFRED ELWES

A dog has one aim in life. . .
to bestow his heart.

J. R. ACKERLEY

He loves us not only in his consciousness
and his intelligence: the very instinct
of his race, the entire unconsciousness
of his species, it appears, think only of us,
dream only of being useful to us.

MAURICE MAETERLINCK

Friendship

Though my dog is my best friend, Lord,
may he never be my only friend. Help me
to build relationships with other dog lovers,
in the dog park, on walks, and by sharing
the joys of having a dog with others.

*For I am persuaded beyond doubt
(am sure) that neither death nor life,
nor angels nor principalities, nor things
impending and threatening nor things to
come, nor powers, nor height nor depth,
nor anything else in all creation will be able
to separate us from the love of God which
is in Christ Jesus our Lord.*

ROMANS 8:38–39 AMP

*Understand, therefore, that the LORD your
God is indeed God. He is the faithful God
who keeps his covenant for a thousand
generations and lavishes his unfailing love on
those who love him and obey his commands.*

DEUTERONOMY 7:9 NLT

I'll be good, really! plead the rescue dog's eyes. You take him home, shower him with affection, train him in your ways. In time, he finally feels loved. One day he empties the trash can on your floor, breaks into the dog treats, and chews six rolls of toilet paper. Congratulations, you've bonded!

PAMELA MCQUADE

[Being a parent] is tough. If you just want a wonderful little creature to love, you can get a puppy.

BARBARA WALTERS

I've caught more ills from people
sneezing over me and giving me virus
infections than from kissing dogs.

BARBARA WOODHOUSE

As much as any animal on earth, dogs
express emotions as purely and clearly
as a five-year-old child, and surely that's
part of why we love them so much.

PATRICIA B. MCCONNELL

Folk will know how large your soul is,
by the way you treat a dog.

CHARLES F. DORAN

That is what the Scriptures mean when they say, "No eye has seen, no ear has heard, and no mind has imagined what God has prepared for those who love him."

1 CORINTHIANS 2:9 NLT

And hope does not put us to shame, because God's love has been poured out into our hearts through the Holy Spirit, who has been given to us.

ROMANS 5:5 NIV

We have confidence in the Lord that you are doing and will continue to do the things we command. May the Lord direct your hearts into God's love and Christ's perseverance.

2 THESSALONIANS 3:4–5 NIV

The relationships between man and dog can often be as complex as that between man and woman. We have, own, or are owned by dogs for a great variety of reasons, not all of them exactly to our credit. We all want to be loved.

IAN NIALL

Ask of the beasts and they will teach you the beauty of this earth.

FRANCIS OF ASSISI

Of the animals who live with us, many are worthy of recognition, and more than all the others and most faithful to man is the dog.

PLINY THE ELDER

Love animals: God has given them the rudiments of thought and joy untroubled. Do not trouble their joy, don't harass them, don't deprive them of their happiness, don't work against God's intent.

FYODOR DOSTOYEVSKY

Children and dogs are as necessary to the welfare of the country as Wall Street and the railroads.

HARRY S. TRUMAN

44

On the Trail

Now the Berean Jews were of more noble character than those in Thessalonica, for they received the message with great eagerness and examined the Scriptures every day to see if what Paul said was true.

ACTS 17:11 NIV

When I was a child, our family had two English springer spaniels. The first one we named Ginger. When she got too old to retrieve game during a hunt, my father bought a puppy we called Max. Once these dogs got the scent of a squirrel, rabbit, or pheasant, off they'd go, following the trail of their quarry. Although they were both terrific and eager trackers, Max turned out to be gun-shy, making him useless on my father's hunting expeditions and a quivering mass of jelly during thunderstorms or fireworks.

Just like a good hunting dog eagerly searches for his master's game, so should we be panting for God's Word, expectantly looking for His message to us, His willing servants. Would that we would not be Word-shy, but fearless followers, anxious to please Him by seeking out His truths, grasping them in our hearts, courageously applying them to our lives, and reveling with joy because we have found and retrieved precious quarry.

Nobody ever saw a dog make a fair and deliberate exchange of one bone for another with another dog. . . . When an animal wants to obtain something. . .it has no other means of persuasion but to gain the favor of those whose services it requires.

Adam Smith

Humankind is drawn to dogs because they are so like ourselves—bumbling, affectionate, confused, easily disappointed, eager to be amused, grateful for kindness and the least attention.

Pam Brown

Smell is supremely important to dogs. . . .
The average dog's nose is about 10,000 to
100,000 times more sensitive than our own.

DAVID TAYLOR

My dog can bark like a congressman,
fetch like an aide, beg like a press
secretary, and play dead like a
receptionist when the phone rings.

U.S. CONGRESSMAN GERALD B. H. SOLOMON

A dog will look at you as if to say, "What do
you want me to do for you? I'll do anything for
you." Whether a dog can in fact, do anything
for you if you don't have sheep (I never have)
is another matter. The dog is willing.

ROY BLOUNT JR.

Everything God says is true—and it's a shield for all who come to him for safety.

PROVERBS 30:5 CEV

I have written to you who are God's children because you know the Father. I have written to you who are mature in the faith because you know Christ, who existed from the beginning. I have written to you who are young in the faith because you are strong. God's word lives in your hearts, and you have won your battle with the evil one.

1 JOHN 2:14 NLT

Pay attention to advice and accept correction, so you can live sensibly.

PROVERBS 19:20 CEV

[Marley] was a master at pursuing his prey. It was the concept of returning it that he did not seem to quite grasp. His general attitude seemed to be, If you want the stick back that bad, YOU jump in the water for it.

JOHN GROGAN

The dog proved rather a doubtful possession .... Its appetite was tremendous, and its preference for my society embarrassingly unrestrained. It would not be content to sleep anywhere else than in my room. . . . [But] part with him I could not; for Bob loved me.

JACOB A. RIIS

Stewardship

Lord, You've given me this dog to care for.
Help me share the loving-kindness I've
received from You. Remind me, when
I'm tired and cranky, that I'm accountable
to You for my care for him.

For whatever was thus written in former days was written for our instruction, that by [our steadfast and patient] endurance and the encouragement [drawn] from the Scriptures we might hold fast to and cherish hope.

Romans 15:4 amp

I want you to recall the words spoken in the past by the holy prophets and the command given by our Lord and Savior through your apostles.

2 Peter 3:2 niv

I'll walk where my own nature would
be leading—It vexes me to choose
another guide.

EMILY BRONTË

For man, "seeing is believing." Well, for a dog,
smelling is believing. If she doesn't smell it,
she can't figure it out. It's not real to her. . . .
Dogs have the ability to sniff out smells that
we can't even pick up using sophisticated
scientific equipment.

CESAR MILLAN

You may have a dog that won't sit up,
roll over, or even cook breakfast, not
because she's too stupid to learn how
but because she's too smart to bother.

RICK HOROWITZ

A dog too, had he; not for need,
But one to play with and to feed;
Which would have led him, if bereft
Of company or friends, and left
Without a better guide.

WILLIAM WORDSWORTH

Training Moment

A well-trained dog is a lifelong pleasure.
Thank You, Lord, for keeping me patient in
teaching my dog how we can share a safe,
happy, and loving life. May I always faithfully
show my dog the best way to live.

*Long ago in many ways and at many times
God's prophets spoke his message to our
ancestors. But now at last, God sent his Son
to bring his message to us. God created
the universe by his Son, and everything will
someday belong to the Son.*

Hebrews 1:1–2 cev

*Your word is a lamp for my feet,
a light on my path.*

Psalm 119:105 niv

*Let the teaching of Christ live in you richly.
Use all wisdom to teach and instruct each
other by singing psalms, hymns, and spiritual
songs with thankfulness in your hearts to God.*

Colossians 3:16 ncv

When you think about it, dogs are incredible creatures. In a short time, they can learn an amazing amount of our human language. . .they have the capacity to intuit our moods, read our facial expressions, and find meaning in our body language.

BASH DIBRA

Patience: That quality of long-suffering a human may not have when he gets a stubborn dog, but that surely will develop over time as the dog completes its people-training program.

PAMELA MCQUADE

My name is Stumps, and my mistress is rather a nice little girl; but she has her faults, like most people. I myself, as it happens, am wonderfully free from faults.

EDITH NESBIT

Whether the Creator planned it so, or environment and human companionship have made it so, men may learn richly through the love and fidelity of a brave and devoted dog.

WARREN G. HARDING

When your words came, I ate them;
they were my joy and my heart's delight,
*for I bear your name, L*ORD *God Almighty.*

JEREMIAH 15:16 NIV

For the word of God is alive and powerful.
It is sharper than the sharpest two-edged
sword, cutting between soul and spirit,
between joint and marrow. It exposes our
innermost thoughts and desires.

HEBREWS 4:12 NLT

Like newborn babies you should crave (thirst
for, earnestly desire) the pure (unadulterated)
spiritual milk, that by it you may be nurtured
and grow unto [completed] salvation.

1 PETER 2:2 AMP

*Seek the L*ORD *while He may be found,*
call upon Him while He is near.

ISAIAH 55:6 NKJV

Master, this is thy Servant.
He is rising eight weeks old.
He is mainly head and tummy.
His legs are uncontrolled.
But thou hast forgiven his ugliness,
and settled him on thy knee...
Art thou content with thy Servant?
He is very comfy with thee.

RUDYARD KIPLING

As terrier he would dig furiously
by the hour after a field mouse;
as spaniel he would "read" the
breeze with the best nose among
the dog folk of our neighborhood,
or follow a trail quite well.

HARRY ESTY DOUNCE

To my way of thinking there's something
wrong, or missing, with any person
who hasn't got a soft spot in their
heart for an animal of some kind.

WILL JAMES

One of the advantages of being
disorderly is that one is constantly
making exciting discoveries.

A. A. MILNE

Security Blanket

He who dwells in the secret place of the Most High shall remain stable and fixed under the shadow of the Almighty. . . . He will cover you with His pinions, and under His wings shall you trust and find refuge. . . . You shall not be afraid. . . .

Psalm 91:1, 4–5 AMP

Our dog Durham, a shar-pei–yellow-lab mixed mutt, is around ninety pounds of pure love and muscle who spends most of his time determined to get his daily eighteen hours of shut-eye. When the ways of the world attempt to disturb his rigorous sleep schedule, he finds solace in his little burgundy, green, and white afghan. This security blanket is able to smooth Durham's hackles raised by strange dogs walking down the sidewalk or a rapid knock on the front door.

We, too, can get our peace disturbed by the unexpected. Thank God for providing us with His unfathomable security. In His all-encompassing presence, wrapped in His infinite arms, we can be at peace. With God as our covering, we need not be afraid but can rest easy no matter what comes down our sidewalk or knocks at our door.

Old dog Tray's ever faithful;
Grief cannot drive him away;
He is gentle, he is kind—
I shall never, never find
A better friend than old dog Tray!

STEPHEN COLLINS FOSTER

An early-morning walk is a
blessing for the whole day.

HENRY DAVID THOREAU

I have been studying the traits and
dispositions of the "lower animals"
(so called) and contrasting them with
the traits and dispositions of man.
I find the result humiliating to me.

MARK TWAIN

If you don't know where you are going,
any road will get you there.

LEWIS CARROLL

All of the animals except man know that the
principal business of life is to enjoy it.

SAMUEL BUTLER

Surely, Lord, you bless the righteous;
you surround them with your
favor as with a shield.

PSALM 5:12 NIV

"The Lord lives! Blessed be my Rock!
Let God be exalted, the Rock of my salvation!"

2 SAMUEL 22:47 NKJV

You have given me your shield of
victory. Your right hand supports
me; your help has made me great.

PSALM 18:35 NLT

The Lord is a mighty tower where
his people can run for safety.

PROVERBS 18:10 CEV

Dogs make us believe we can
actually be as they see us.

THE MONKS OF NEW SKETE

Dogs need to do something. They want to
feel useful. They love to work for praise and
to feel accomplished. Sitting around and
decorating the hearth isn't quite enough.
Tricks can be a useful and entertaining
addition to your dog's education.

CAPTAIN ARTHUR J. HAGGERTY
AND CAROL LEA BENJAMIN

Short Days

Thank You, Lord, for my lively little pup.
Remind me that these days of puppyhood
are short. Give me large doses of patience
and love, along with enough determination
to train her for a lifetime.

*We wait in hope for the LORD;
he is our help and our shield.*

PSALM 33:20 NIV

*Every word of God is pure: he is a shield
unto them that put their trust in him.*

PROVERBS 30:5 KJV

*He will cover you with his feathers,
and under his wings you can hide.
His truth will be your shield and protection.*

PSALM 91:4 NCV

*"But whoever listens to me will live in safety
and be at ease, without fear of harm."*

PROVERBS 1:33 NIV

Some humans love terriers, others
retrievers; some adore sheepdogs,
while others cotton up to hounds.
Like dogs, people are all different,
but there's a breed for any one of us.

PAMELA MCQUADE

This honest sheep-dog's countenance I read;
With him can talk; nor blush to waste a word
On creatures less intelligent and shrewd.

WILLIAM WORDSWORTH

Extremely smart dogs are typically
very challenging pets because they learn
not just what you want them to learn,
but all sorts of other things as well. They
are very observant. . .which is why they
sometimes seem to read our minds.

KIM SAUNDERS

When living seems but little worth
And all things go awry,
I close the door, we journey forth—
My dog and I! . . .

And ere we reach the busy town,
Like birds my troubles fly,
We are two comrades glad of heart—
My dog and I!

ALICE J. CLEATOR

Wondrous Design

Lord, You've helped me appreciate
how wondrously You've made the dog.
Out of all the animals You made,
this one was designed as my special
companion and friend. Thank You.

He said: The Lord is my Rock [of escape from Saul] and my Fortress [in the wilderness] and my Deliverer; My God, my Rock, in Him will I take refuge; my Shield and the Horn of my salvation; my Stronghold and my Refuge, my Savior—You save me from violence. I call on the Lord, Who is worthy to be praised, and I am saved from my enemies.

2 Samuel 22:2–4 amp

Be my mighty rock, the place where I can always run for protection. Save me by your command! You are my mighty rock and my fortress.

Psalm 71:3 cev

All dogs are great opportunists.
That's important to remember when you try
to teach your puppy the rules of the house.

JOHN ROSS AND BARBARA McKINNEY

How beautiful it is to do nothing,
and then rest afterward.

DANISH PROVERB

True obedience is true freedom.

HENRY WARD BEECHER

I used to look at [my dog] Smokey and think, "If you were a little smarter you could tell me what you were thinking," and he'd look at me like he was saying, "If you were a little smarter, I wouldn't have to."

FRED JUNGCLAUS

Dogs come when they're called. Cats take a message and get back to you.

MARY BLY

Puppy parenting is not about buying the best of everything. It is about providing the best care and giving lots of love.

JAN GREYE AND GAIL SMITH WITH BEVERLY BEYETTE

*Behold, the Lord God will come with
might, and His arm will rule for Him.
Behold, His reward is with Him,
and His recompense before Him.*

ISAIAH 40:10 AMP

*"When you go through deep waters, I will
be with you. When you go through rivers of
difficulty, you will not drown. When you walk
through the fire of oppression, you will not be
burned up; the flames will not consume you."*

ISAIAH 43:2 NLT

*The LORD is a shelter for the oppressed,
a refuge in times of trouble.*

PSALM 9:9 NLT

His long-tried friend, for they,
As well we knew, together had grown grey.
The Master died, his drooping servant's grief
Found at the widow's feet some sad relief;
Yet still he lived in pining discontent,
Sadness which no indulgence could prevent.

William Wordsworth

Confront a child, a puppy, and a kitten
with a sudden danger; the child will
turn instinctively for assistance,
the puppy will grovel in abject
submission, the kitten will brace its
tiny body for a frantic resistance.

SAKI

Action may not always bring happiness. . .
but there is no happiness without action.

BENJAMIN DISRAELI

People bond with their dogs by creating
a happy environment. . . . The key to
being a successful dog owner is your
emotional relationship with the animal.

MORDECAI SIEGAL AND MATTHEW MARGOLIS

No Greater
Friend

*A man who has friends must himself
be friendly, but there is a friend
who sticks closer than a brother.*

PROVERBS 18:24 NKJV

Whenever I had a problem as a child, I always found a patient and willing listener in my springer spaniel named Max. As we sat on the living room floor, Max would listen attentively while I told him about my being snubbed by a friend, getting a not-so-good grade, or getting cut from the basketball team.

Yes, dogs are definitely man's (and woman's) best friends, for not only do they have great listening skills and are always willing to lick your tears away, but most will stay by your side through field and forest. Some dogs have even been known to rescue their owners from deadly danger!

The truth is we have an even greater friend in Jesus. There is absolutely no better companion or champion in our lives than He. Jesus, by sacrificing His own life, has already saved us from the ultimate peril—life (and death) without God. And, although dogs may come and go, Jesus, the man who names us as His friends, will stick with us to the very end. What a friend!

Dogs will be fairly indifferent to most
people and pick one, and say,
"That's the person I'll work for."

NINA BONDARENKO

Why own a dog?
There's a danger you know,
You can't own just one,
for the craving will grow.
There's no doubt they're addictive,
wherein lies the danger.
While living with lots,
you'll grow poorer and stranger.

UNKNOWN

What dogs? These are my children,
little people with fur who make
my heart open a little wider.

OPRAH WINFREY

Constantly chain a dog to a tree, and he'll
become vicious. Loosely knot him to a heart,
and faithful love will earn his adoration.

PAMELA McQUADE

Living on your own is lonely. Eventually,
you may start thinking about a dog. . . .
But can you care for the needs of a dog?. . .
Before you adopt that puppy, be sure you
are ready for a fifteen-year commitment.

TONI SORTOR

*Your kingdom is an everlasting kingdom,
and your dominion endures through all
generations. The Lord is trustworthy in all
he promises and faithful in all he does. The
Lord upholds all who fall and lifts up all who
are bowed down. The eyes of all look to you,
and you give them their food at the proper
time. You open your hand and satisfy the
desires of every living thing.*

PSALM 145:13–16 NIV

*Cast your burden on the Lord, and He
shall sustain you; He shall never
permit the righteous to be moved.*

PSALM 55:22 NKJV

A little dog that wags his tail
And knows no other joy,
Of such a little dog am I
Reminded by a boy

Who gambols all the living day
Without an earthly cause,
Because he is a little boy
I honestly suppose.

EMILY DICKINSON

Best Friends

Thank You, Lord, for the joys of having a dog.
Help me to find enough time to play with
him, walk him, and care for him. May he not
only be my best friend, may I be his.

My old self has been crucified with Christ.
It is no longer I who live, but Christ lives
in me. So I live in this earthly body by
trusting in the Son of God, who loved
me and gave himself for me.

GALATIANS 2:20 NLT

Know, recognize, and understand therefore
this day and turn your [mind and] heart to it
that the Lord is God in the heavens above and
upon the earth beneath; there is no other.

DEUTERONOMY 4:39 AMP

"But will God really dwell on earth?
The heavens, even the highest heaven,
cannot contain you. How much less
this temple I have built!"

1 KINGS 8:27 NIV

Drop a towel, quilt, pillows, or bedsheets on the floor, and a dog will easily decide it's a wonderful, soft bed that has the additional quality of smelling just like her favorite human.

PAMELA MCQUADE

The only way to have a friend is to be one.

RALPH WALDO EMERSON

The great pleasure of a dog is that you may make a fool of yourself with him and not only will he not scold you, but he will make a fool of himself, too.

SAMUEL BUTLER

I am a much better person
with a dog in my lap.

John O'Hurley

Dogs have a way of finding the people
who need them, filling an emptiness
we don't even know we have.

Thom Jones

Thanks, Lord!

Thank You, Lord, for giving me a dog who reminds me of the joy in life. When people depress me with bad news, my dog points out that there's still reason to remain cheerful: we still have each other and a good game of ball.

Cast me not away from Your presence and
take not Your Holy Spirit from me.

PSALM 51:11 AMP

"Abide in Me, and I in you. As the branch
cannot bear fruit of itself, unless it abides in
the vine, neither can you, unless you abide in
Me. I am the vine, you are the branches. He
who abides in Me, and I in him, bears much
fruit; for without Me you can do nothing."

JOHN 15:4–5 NKJV

"If we are not faithful, he will still be faithful.
Christ cannot deny who he is."

2 TIMOTHY 2:13 CEV

Archie's seven-week-old St. Bernard
puppy has come and it is the dearest
puppy imaginable; a huge, soft thing,
which Archie carries around in his arms
and which the whole family loves.

THEODORE ROOSEVELT

If your dog is fat,
you're not getting enough exercise.

UNKNOWN

Dogs feel very strongly that they should always go with you in the car, in case the need should arise for them to bark violently at nothing right in your ear.

DAVE BARRY

Some of my best leading men have been dogs and horses.

ELIZABETH TAYLOR

"Home is where the heart is" until the humans walk out the door. That's when the dog begins to realize that part of the pack is gone. The howling that results may be terrible to hear!

PAMELA MCQUADE

Again Jesus said, "Peace be with you! As the Father has sent me, I am sending you." And with that he breathed on them and said, "Receive the Holy Spirit."

JOHN 20:21–22 NIV

"But you will receive power when the Holy Spirit comes upon you. And you will be my witnesses, telling people about me everywhere—in Jerusalem, throughout Judea, in Samaria, and to the ends of the earth."

ACTS 1:8 NLT

There is no one in all the Great World
more faithful than a faithful dog.

THORNTON W. BURGESS

Pray steal me not, I'm Mrs. Dingley's,
Whose heart in this four-footed thing lies.

JONATHAN SWIFT

Not Carnegie, Vanderbilt, and Astor together
could have raised money enough to buy
a quarter share in my little dog.

ERNEST THOMPSON SETON

Those who bring sunshine into
the lives of others, cannot
keep it from themselves.

JAMES M. BARRIE

To call him a dog hardly seems to do him
justice, though inasmuch as he had four
legs, a tail, and barked, I admit he was,
to all outward appearances. But to those
of us who knew him well, he was
a perfect gentleman.

HERMIONE GINGOLD

Stay is a charming word
in a friend's vocabulary.

LOUISA MAY ALCOTT

Upon Reflection

For if anyone only listens to the Word without obeying it and being a doer of it, he is like a man who looks carefully at his [own] natural face in a mirror; for he thoughtfully observes himself, and then goes off and promptly forgets what he was like.

JAMES 1:23–24 AMP

As a puppy, Durham had an amazingly elusive nemesis. He was only seen when Durham stood in front of our stove and gazed into its window. That's because Durham's rival was his own reflection! He panted when Durham panted, whined when he whined, and barked when he barked. What a strange creature! And how frustrating for Durham that he could never reach him!

Fortunately, we humans are a bit smarter than dogs. We know that the face we see in the mirror (or stove window) is actually our own. But are we seeing a soon-to-be-forgotten reflection or our true selves in the light of God's Word?

James advises us to look carefully at scripture and then study ourselves, content not just with hearing how we are to be conformed to Christ's image but actually making the changes and improvements God wants us to make—without whining or barking. That's something to reflect on.

If you think dogs can't count, try putting three
dog biscuits in your pocket and
then giving Fido only two of them.

PHIL PASTORET

Mother is going to present Gem to Uncle Will.
. . . Gem is really a very nice small bow-wow,
but Mother found that in this case possession
was less attractive than pursuit. When she
takes him out walking, he carries her along
as if she were a Roman chariot.

THEODORE ROOSEVELT

I care not much for a man's religion whose
dog and cat are not the better for it.

ABRAHAM LINCOLN

A door is what a dog is perpetually
on the wrong side of.

Ogden Nash

Once your new dog gets used to your
schedule, don't be surprised if he wakes
you in the morning. Canines don't need
a clock to know what hour it is.

Pamela McQuade

A house without either a cat or
a dog is the house of a scoundrel.

Portuguese Proverb

If a dog will not come to you after having
looked you in the face, you should go
home and examine your conscience.

Woodrow Wilson

The dog has got more fun out of man than man has got out of the dog, for the clearly demonstrable reason that man is the more laughable of the two animals.

JAMES THURBER

The one absolute, unselfish friend that a man can have in this selfish world—the one that never deserts him, the one that never proves ungrateful or treacherous—is his dog.

GEORGE GRAHAM VEST

The pattern was always the same, Dan stretched on the passenger seat with his head on my knee, Hector peering through the windshield, his paws balanced on my hand as it rested on the gear lever. . . . Hector hated to miss a thing.

JAMES HERRIOT

"For I know the plans I have for you," declares the LORD, *"plans to prosper you and not to harm you, plans to give you hope and a future."*

JEREMIAH 29:11 NIV

"If this is true, let me know what your plans are, then I can obey and continue to please you. And don't forget that you have chosen this nation to be your own." The LORD said, "I will go with you and give you peace."

EXODUS 33:13–14 CEV

Canine Vision

Help me, Lord, to sometimes see life
through my dog's eyes. May I appreciate
the joy of greeting someone I love and
delight in the cool morning breeze
as we take a long walk together.

You said to me, "I will point out the road that you should follow. I will be your teacher and watch over you."

PSALM 32:8 CEV

For that is what God is like. He is our God forever and ever, and he will guide us until we die.

PSALM 48:14 NLT

Your kingdom is an everlasting kingdom, and Your dominion endures throughout all generations. The LORD upholds all who fall, and raises up all who are bowed down.

PSALM 145:13–14 NKJV

The censure of a dog is something
no man can stand.

CHRISTOPHER MORLEY

The factory of the future will have
only two employees, a man and a dog.
The man will be there to feed the dog.
The dog will be there to keep the man
from touching the equipment.

WARREN G. BENNIS

If you get to thinking you're a person
of some influence, try ordering
somebody else's dog around.

WILL ROGERS

For an animal person,
an animal-less home is no home at all.

CLEVELAND AMORY

If dogs were fashioned out of men
What breed of dog would I have been?
And would I e'er deserve caress,
Or be extolled for faithfulness
Like my dog here?

JOSEPH M. ANDERSON

It's funny how dogs and cats know the insides
of folks better than other folks do, isn't it?

ELEANOR H. PORTER

Do not fret or have any anxiety about anything, but in every circumstance and in everything, by prayer and petition (definite requests), with thanksgiving, continue to make your wants known to God. And God's peace [shall be yours, that tranquil state of a soul assured of its salvation through Christ, and so fearing nothing from God and being content with its earthly lot of whatever sort that is, that peace] which transcends all understanding shall garrison and mount guard over your hearts and minds in Christ Jesus.

PHILIPPIANS 4:6–7 AMP

Fur Count

Lord, thank You for the deep dog–human
bond. May people who have lost their
beloved companions be comforted by
Your deep love and know that not one
bit of fur was uncounted by You.

Lad did not belong to the howling type.
When he was unhappy, he waxed silent.
And his sorrowful eyes took on a deeper woe.
By the way, if there is anything more sorrowful
than the eyes of a collie pup that has never
known sorrow, I have yet to see it.

ALBERT PAYSON TERHUNE

It is verily a great thing to live in obedience,
to be under authority, and not to be at
our own disposal. Far safer is it to live in
subjection than in a place of authority.

THOMAS À KEMPIS

An animal's eyes have the
power to speak a great language.

MARTIN BUBER

[Mungo] was a medium-sized dog, nothing
special, a hound of some sort, the kind
you'd pick out at the shelter to adopt, flop-
eared, tan and white coat, immediately
likeable, the kind of dog you itched to
scratch between the ears.

MARTHA GRIMES

I tell you not to worry about your life. Don't worry about having something to eat, drink, or wear. Isn't life more than food or clothing? Look at the birds in the sky! They don't plant or harvest. They don't even store grain in barns. Yet your Father in heaven takes care of them. Aren't you worth more than birds?

MATTHEW 6:25–26 CEV

And the Lord your God will make you abundantly prosperous in every work of your hand, in the fruit of your body, of your cattle, of your land, for good; for the Lord will again delight in prospering you, as He took delight in your fathers.

DEUTERONOMY 30:9 AMP

What bliss it is to rub the soft fur atop the ear of a long-eared hound or gently touch the tender fur of a puppy.

PAMELA MCQUADE

Puppies need toys as much as kids do, and they should learn that it's good to pick up and play—as roughly as they want—with these toys and not with hands. Hands are for stroking, petting, and for making your dog feel good, not for chewing.

JOHN C. WRIGHT WITH JUDI WRIGHT LASHNITS

Most puppies, at one time or another, will have a go at landscape gardening. Leave your puppy outside on his own for long periods and he will get into mischief, just as a toddler would.

TERRY RYAN AND THERESA SHIPP

Never put off till tomorrow the fun you can have today.

ALDOUS HUXLEY

Although you may feel a little silly, it's well worth going round every room in the house on all fours, to see exactly what is within reach of an inquisitive, playful puppy!

DAVID TAYLOR

"Deaf" Takes
a Holiday

Not one of you has ever given ear to His [God's] voice or seen His form (His face—what He is like). [You have always been deaf to His voice and blind to the vision of Him.]

JOHN 5:37 AMP

Our springer spaniels, Max and Ginger, both went deaf in their old age. Fortunately, we could still communicate with them. First we would clap our hands to get their attention. Once their eyes were on us, we used hand signals for commands to stay, come, sit, and shake.

Sometimes we ourselves are deaf when it comes to God's voice. We allow our ears to be filled with the clamor of the world. During those times, God sometimes makes a loud noise to get our attention. At Jesus' baptism, God's voice boomed, telling the world Jesus was His beloved Son. But even after that miraculous message, people still did not hear. For the apostle Paul, God went to extremes with not only a mighty voice but a blinding flash from heaven.

If you haven't heard God's voice lately, try tuning out the world long enough to give Him your total and complete attention. Allow "deaf" to take a holiday by opening your ears to His Word.

My hounds are bred out
of the Spartan kind,
So flew'd, so sanded,
and their heads are hung
With ears that sweep
away the morning dew;
Crook-knee'd, and dew-lapp'd
like Thessalian bulls;
Slow in pursuit, but match'd
in mouth like bells,
Each under each.

WILLIAM SHAKESPEARE

God will prepare everything for our perfect happiness in heaven, and if it takes my dog being there, I believe he'll be there.

BILLY GRAHAM

Be thou comforted, little dog, thou too in resurrection shall have a little golden tail.

MARTIN LUTHER

We treat our dogs as if they were "almost human": that is why they really become "almost human" in the end.

C. S. LEWIS

Stop worrying about the potholes in the road and celebrate the journey!

BARBARA HOFFMAN

As bad as you are, you still know how to give good gifts to your children. But your heavenly Father is even more ready to give good things to people who ask.

MATTHEW 7:11 CEV

Listen to my words, LORD, consider my lament. Hear my cry for help, my King and my God, for to you I pray. In the morning, LORD, you hear my voice; in the morning I lay my requests before you and wait expectantly.

PSALM 5:1–3 NIV

Morning, noon, and night I cry out in my distress, and the LORD hears my voice.

PSALM 55:17 NLT

It was the Great Creator Himself who made dogs too human—so human that sometimes they put humanity to shame.

LAURENCE HUTTON

If a dog jumps in your lap, it is because he is fond of you; but if a cat does the same thing, it is because your lap is warmer.

ALFRED NORTH WHITEHEAD

Forgiveness

Lord, my dog may not be perfect,
but I still love her. Help me to
encourage her and focus on the things
she does right. Remind me, as anger
threatens, that when I fail, You still love me.

Listen to my words, Lord, consider my lament. Hear my cry for help, my King and my God, for to you I pray. In the morning, Lord, you hear my voice; in the morning I lay my requests before you and wait expectantly.

PSALM 5:1–3 NIV

"Even he rendered a just decision in the end. So don't you think God will surely give justice to his chosen people who cry out to him day and night? Will he keep putting them off?"

LUKE 18:7 NLT

Rejoicing in hope, patient in tribulation, continuing steadfastly in prayer. . .

ROMANS 12:12 NKJV

Dogs are better than human beings
because they know but do not tell.

EMILY DICKINSON

The most affectionate creature
in the whole world is a wet dog.

AMBROSE BIERCE

Let God's Word and God's love be
the herd dogs chasing your thoughts
into the prayer corral.

CHUCK MILLER

Before her home, in her accustom'd seat,
The tidy Grandam spins beneath the shade
Of the old honeysuckle, at her feet
The dreaming pug, and purring tabby laid.

FREDERICK TENNYSON

It is true that animals play an important
role in prose fiction, more important
than is often realized, for a book without
animals is seldom a living book.

CARL VAN VECHTEN

If My people, who are called by My name, shall humble themselves, pray, seek, crave, and require of necessity My face and turn from their wicked ways, then will I hear from heaven, forgive their sin, and heal their land.

2 Chronicles 7:14 amp

"Then you will call my name. You will come to me and pray to me, and I will listen to you. You will search for me. And when you search for me with all your heart, you will find me!"

Jeremiah 29:12–13 ncv

Appreciation

Lord, I give my dog a simple dog treat,
and he acts as if he's received a five-course
dinner. May I be that appreciative of the
ordinary, good things You give me.

It was necessary. . .to convince yourself
that it is vain to pursue birds who fly away
and that you are unable to clamber up
trees after the cats who defy you there; to
distinguish between the sunny spots where
it is delicious to sleep and the patches
of shade in which you shiver.

MAURICE MAETERLINCK

When they come to live with us, dogs never look at the size of our homes. They only judge us by the size of our hearts.

PAMELA MCQUADE

No squirrel went abroad;
A dog's belated feet
Like intermittent plush were heard
Adown the empty street.

EMILY DICKINSON

In the spring, at the end of the day, you should smell like dirt.

MARGARET ATWOOD

So let us come boldly to the throne of our gracious God. There we will receive his mercy, and we will find grace to help us when we need it most.

HEBREWS 4:16 NLT

The LORD detests the sacrifice of the wicked, but he delights in the prayers of the upright.

PROVERBS 15:8 NLT

I will provide for their needs before they ask, and I will help them while they are still asking for help.

ISAIAH 65:24 NCV

His mistress once praised him for bringing home a pretty lace handkerchief he had found on the highway. Until I forbade any further gifts, [Sunnybank Robert] bore to her every roadside offering he could find: a car crank, an umbrella with a Chinese sword handle, a devastatingly dead chicken, and an equally flattened skunk.

ALBERT PAYSON TERHUNE

For though he had very little Latin beyond "Cave canem [beware of the dog]," he had, as a young dog, devoured Shakespeare (in a tasty leather binding).

DODIE SMITH

It's not the size of the dog in the fight,
it's the size of the fight in the dog.

MARK TWAIN

Youngsters of the age of two
and three are endowed
with extraordinary strength.
They can lift a dog twice
their own weight and dump
him into the bathtub.

ERMA BOMBECK

One reason a dog can be such a
comfort when you're feeling blue is
that he doesn't try to find out why.

UNKNOWN

Learning by
Example

*Pattern yourselves after me
[follow my example], as I imitate
and follow Christ (the Messiah).*

1 Corinthians 11:1 AMP

When Max joined our family, Ginger was not happy with the new kid on her block. But she did find a way to tolerate him. Eager to please, Max followed Ginger everywhere and imitated everything she did. That included squatting to relieve himself instead of lifting his leg like others of his gender. Max's problem was that there was no male dog in his realm from which he could learn boy dog behavior.

As Christians, we are called to pattern our lives after Christ. But sometimes we, too, deviate from the example that God has set before us and end up imitating the sinful instead of the Savior. That's because when our eyes are on the temporal instead of the spiritual, we wind up on the wrong path, looking to please people instead of God.

To stay in focus and on the right road, keep your eyes on Jesus. Following His example, you'll find true relief.

I have a dog of Blenheim birth,
With fine long ears and full of mirth;
And sometimes, running o'er the plain,
He tumbles on his nose:
But quickly jumping up again,
Like lightning on he goes!

JOHN RUSKIN

As you're raising your puppy, keep an eye on what you want her to be in the future. Behaviors such as nipping or barking, which seem cute in a puppy, could be disastrous in an adult dog.

PAMELA MCQUADE

The impact of gentle handling can be seen even if it occurs before birth: puppies born to mothers who were petted during pregnancy tend to be more receptive to handling after birth.

PATRICIA B. MCCONNELL

No philosophers so thoroughly comprehend us as dogs and horses.

HERMAN MELVILLE

God is awesome in his sanctuary. The God of Israel gives power and strength to his people. Praise be to God!

PSALM 68:35 NLT

My body and mind may fail, but you are my strength and my choice forever.

PSALM 73:26 CEV

"The righteous keep moving forward, and those with clean hands become stronger and stronger."

JOB 17:9 NLT

That you may walk worthy of the Lord, fully pleasing Him, being fruitful in every good work and increasing in the knowledge of God; strengthened with all might, according to His glorious power, for all patience and longsuffering with joy. . .

COLOSSIANS 1:10–11 NKJV

The master talked of buying a whalebone-and-steel-and-snow bull terrier, or a more formidable if more greedy Great Dane. But the mistress wanted a collie. So they compromised by getting the collie.

ALBERT PAYSON TERHUNE

Go with the Flow

Lord, I know my dog was bred for a certain purpose, and I can't change those inbred traits, no matter how hard I try. Help me to accept those things I can't change, develop his good points, and love him no matter what.

In conclusion, be strong in the Lord [be empowered through your union with Him]; draw your strength from Him [that strength which His boundless might provides]. Put on God's whole armor [the armor of a heavy-armed soldier which God supplies], that you may be able successfully to stand up against [all] the strategies and the deceits of the devil.

EPHESIANS 6:10–11 AMP

Each time he said, "My grace is all you need. My power works best in weakness." So now I am glad to boast about my weaknesses, so that the power of Christ can work through me.

2 CORINTHIANS 12:9 NLT

One learns to itch
where one can scratch.

ERNEST BRAMAH

The upper half of the door was of glass and,
as I peered through, a river of dogs poured
round the corner of a long passage and
dashed itself with frenzied yells against the
door. If I hadn't been used to animals I would
have turned and run for my life.

JAMES HERRIOT

I can feel the wind go by when I run.
It feels good. It feels fast.

EVELYN ASHFORD

A Dog's Perspective: Eat a live toad the first
thing in the morning and nothing worse
will happen to you the rest of the day.

U N K N O W N

Home and Love

Lord, I often hear about dogs who don't
have homes. Help me do my part to help
those homeless companions find the
people who will love them.

He was amazed to see that no one intervened to help the oppressed. So he himself stepped in to save them with his strong arm, and his justice sustained him. He put on righteousness as his body armor and placed the helmet of salvation on his head. He clothed himself with a robe of vengeance and wrapped himself in a cloak of divine passion.

ISAIAH 59:16–17 NLT

The word of the LORD came to Abram in a vision, saying, "Do not be afraid, Abram. I am your shield, your exceedingly great reward."

GENESIS 15:1–2 NKJV

A vigorous five-mile walk will do more good for an unhappy, but otherwise healthy adult than all the medicine and psychology in the world.

PAUL DUDLEY WHITE

I want to walk through life instead of being dragged through it.

ALANIS MORISSETTE

Don't you wonder just what your dogs do when they're home alone? Do they sleep on the forbidden couch, chew on a toy, or climb onto the table? Or maybe they curl up in their own beds or in the hallway and dream of your return.

PAMELA MCQUADE

Joy will make a puppy of an old dog.

THORNTON W. BURGESS

Seek home for rest, for home is best.

THOMAS TUSSER

*If this is so, then the Lord knows how
to rescue the godly from trials and
to hold the unrighteous for punishment
on the day of judgment.*

2 PETER 2:9 NIV

*"Watch and pray, lest you enter into
temptation. The spirit indeed is willing,
but the flesh is weak."*

MATTHEW 26:41 NKJV

*The only temptation that has come to you is
that which everyone has. But you can trust
God, who will not permit you to be tempted
more than you can stand. But when you are
tempted, he will also give you a way to escape
so that you will be able to stand it.*

1 CORINTHIANS 10:13 NCV

150

In summer, when the days were long,
We walk'd, two friends, in field and wood;
Our heart was light, our step was strong,
And life lay round us, fair as good,
In summer, when the days were long.

WATHEN MARKS WILKS CALL

Home, the spot of earth supremely blest,
A dearer, sweeter spot than all the rest.

ROBERT MONTGOMERY

Isn't it amazing how powerful a dog
becomes as soon as it stretches out
on the human's bed? A fifty-pound,
dead-weight dog can take up more
space than the average woman.
He'll also make her apologize for
wanting more than a quarter of
the bed for her own use.

PAMELA McQUADE

Nothing to Fear

The Lord is my light and my salvation—whom shall I fear? The Lord is the stronghold of my life—of whom shall I be afraid?

Psalm 27:1 niv

Durham barks as if he is fearless. Yet there are times when he is anything but.

One day my husband, Pete, brought a huge roll of bubble wrap home. He placed it in our son's room with the intention of using it as packing material to ship something the next day. Later, sitting downstairs, we heard Durham growling on the floor above. My curiosity piqued, I went to the landing, looked up at the top of the steps, and saw Durham halfway into Zach's room, his hackles raised. Alarmed, I ran upstairs and comforted a now-cowering dog. Then, not knowing what I might find, I cautiously peeked into the room. Everything looked normal except for the bubble wrap. As it turned out, that's what had freaked out our ninety-pound, muscle-bound dog!

Sometimes we, too, growl at the things we fear—then cower in fright. But God has told us He's with us through everything! With Him, we have nothing to be afraid of. We can face bubble wrap with courage, knowing that God is our stronghold.

There is only one smartest dog
in the world, and every boy has it.

UNKNOWN

Study hard, and you might grow up to be
president. But let's face it: Even then, you'll
never make as much money as your dog.

GEORGE H. W. BUSH

Everyone enjoys doing the kind
of work for which he is best suited.

NAPOLEON HILL

If it wasn't for dogs, some people
would never go for a walk.

UNKNOWN

The God who made giraffes, a baby's
fingernails, a puppy's tail, a crooknecked
squash, the bobwhite's call, and a young
girl's giggle has a sense of humor.
Make no mistake about that.

CATHERINE MARSHALL

*Above all else, you must live in a way that
brings honor to the good news about Christ.
Then, whether I visit you or not, I will hear
that all of you think alike. I will know that
you are working together and that you are
struggling side by side to get others to believe
the good news. Be brave when you face your
enemies. Your courage will show them that
they are going to be destroyed, and it will
show you that you will be saved.*

PHILIPPIANS 1:27–28 CEV

*Wait on the LORD: be of good courage,
and he shall strengthen thine heart:
wait, I say, on the LORD.*

PSALM 27:14 KJV

I don't eat anything that a dog won't eat.
Like sushi. Ever see a dog eat sushi?
He just sniffs it and says, "I don't think so."
And this is an animal that licks between
its legs and sniffs fire hydrants.

BILLIAM CORONEL

I can train any dog in five minutes.
It's training the owner that takes longer.

BARBARA WOODHOUSE

A Rescuer's Prayer

Lord, I wish I could wrap my arms around
every dog that needs a home. Help me
rescue every dog I can and to remember
that You hold them all fast, because
they all come from Your arms.

*When I asked for your help, you answered
my prayer and gave me courage.*

PSALM 138:3 CEV

*And now, dear children, remain in
fellowship with Christ so that when he
returns, you will be full of courage and
not shrink back from him in shame.*

1 JOHN 2:28 NLT

*So we say with confidence, "The Lord
is my helper; I will not be afraid.
What can mere mortals do to me?"*

HEBREWS 13:6 NIV

*Be strong and take heart,
all you who hope in the LORD.*

PSALM 31:24 NIV

For Christmas 2005, the White House produced the video "A Very Beazley Christmas." Miss Beazley, the Scottish terrier President George W. Bush had bought for his wife that year, received so much attention and praise that their first Scottie, Barney, jealously began hiding Beazley's Christmas presents.

According to the *Guinness Book of World Records*, an American bloodhound named Tigger has the longest dog ears on record. Each of these amazing appendages is well over thirteen inches in length.

I sometimes think I'd rather be a dog and bay at the moon than stay in the Senate another six years and listen to it.

SENATOR JOHN SHARP WILLIAMS

Any man who does not like dogs and want them about does not deserve to be in the White House.

CALVIN COOLIDGE

Two Species

Lord, You have placed this helpless puppy in my arms. As two very different species, we're likely to have communication gaps. Please help me appreciate my dog, and nurture growth and understanding between us.

I have told you these things, so that in Me you may have [perfect] peace and confidence. In the world you have tribulation and trials and distress and frustration; but be of good cheer [take courage; be confident, certain, undaunted]! For I have overcome the world. [I have deprived it of power to harm you and have conquered it for you.]

JOHN 16:33 AMP

After this prayer, the meeting place shook, and they were all filled with the Holy Spirit. Then they preached the word of God with boldness.

ACTS 4:31 NLT

Ellie. . .a shaggy brown Disney-cute mutt, was the West Hebron town dog. She wandered from one house to another, monitoring traffic in and out of the variety store. Sometimes she napped in the middle of Route 30. . . . She belonged to everyone and no one.

JON KATZ

Strangers are just friends waiting to happen.

UNKNOWN

Those who will play with cats
must expect to be scratched.

MIGUEL DE CERVANTES

It's easy to see dogs are popular in
English-speaking nations by looking at
this sampling of words or expressions that
relate to them: top dog, legal beagle, dog in
the manger, shaggy-dog story, dog paddle,
dog-and-pony show, dogged, dog-ear,
dogface, hot dog, dog days, sea dog. . .

PAMELA McQUADE

Cat's Motto: No matter what
you've done wrong, always try to
make it look like the dog did it.

UNKNOWN

167

This is the confidence we have in approaching God: that if we ask anything according to his will, he hears us.

1 JOHN 5:14 NIV

"These things I have spoken to you, that in Me you may have peace. In the world you will have tribulation; but be of good cheer, I have overcome the world."

JOHN 16:33 NKJV

But Jesus immediately said to them: "Take courage! It is I. Don't be afraid."

MATTHEW 14:27 NIV

"But blessed are those who trust in the LORD and have made the LORD their hope and confidence."

JEREMIAH 17:7 NLT

Punch loved everybody. . . . He was as cordial to a beggar as he would have been to a king; and if thieves had come to break through and steal, Punch. . .would have escorted them through the house, and shown them where the treasures were kept.

LAURENCE HUTTON

Labradors are lousy watchdogs. They usually bark when there is a stranger about, but it is an expression of unmitigated joy at the chance to meet somebody new, not a warning.

NORMAN STRUNG

Sleep till you're hungry, eat till you're sleepy.

UNKNOWN

Food is our common ground,
a universal experience.

JAMES BEARD

One cannot think well, love well,
sleep well, if one has not dined well.

VIRGINIA WOOLF

170

*And he did rescue us from mortal
danger, and he will rescue us again.
We have placed our confidence in him,
and he will continue to rescue us.*

2 Corinthians 1:10 NLT

*But you, Lord, are a shield around me,
my glory, the One who lifts my head high.*

Psalm 3:3 NIV

*In his kindness God called you to share in
his eternal glory by means of Christ Jesus.
So after you have suffered a little while,
he will restore, support, and strengthen you,
and he will place you on a firm foundation.*

1 Peter 5:10 NLT

As fly the shadows o'er the grass,
He flies with step as light and sure,
He hunts the wolf through Tostan pass,
And starts the deer by Lisanoure.
The music of the Sabbath bells,
O Con! has not a sweeter sound
Than when along the valley swells
The cry of John Mac Donnell's hound.

DENIS FLORENCE MACCARTHY

Dog Speak

We do not know what we ought to pray for, but the Spirit himself intercedes for us through wordless groans. And he who searches our hearts knows the mind of the Spirit, because the Spirit intercedes for God's people in accordance with the will of God.

ROMANS 8:26–27 NIV

Durham has trouble telling us what he wants. That's because he has the same bark when requesting his bone as he has for requesting kibble, water, carrots, permission to get up on the couch, and access to the outside facilities. So, whenever he barks, we have to offer each item, one at a time, until we hit upon his actual desire.

Sometimes, we, too, have trouble communicating. It can even happen in our prayers to God. Certain situations come up in life and we don't know how to handle them. We aren't even sure exactly how to pray. Fortunately, God has provided us with the Holy Spirit. He can interpret any request we have on our heart—even if we ourselves don't know how to express it!

If only we had such an interpreter to translate our dog's barks, groans, and whines. Where is Doctor Dolittle when you need him?

On a popular dog-intelligence-rating scale, the bloodhound comes in well below the "smart" rating. But ask any human if he'd rather have the top-smarts-rated border collie scent out his missing child, and he'd surely prefer that "stupid" bloodhound's top-rated nose!

PAMELA MCQUADE

How very unlike are poodles and greyhounds! Yet they are of one species.

ADAM SEDGWICK

Golf seems to be an arduous way to go for a walk. I prefer to take the dogs out.

PRINCESS ANNE

Leash: A long, weblike device that allows a dog to control his human and pull her in the opposite direction of where she would otherwise go.

UNKNOWN

Whenever I hear a dog continually barking, my reaction is one of relief that it's not my dog making all that racket and inciting the neighbors to call the police.

JOHN MCCARTHY

The heart is deceitful above all things and beyond cure. Who can understand it? "I the Lord search the heart and examine the mind, to reward each person according to their conduct, according to what their deeds deserve."

JEREMIAH 17:9–10 NIV

In certain ways we are weak, but the Spirit is here to help us. For example, when we don't know what to pray for, the Spirit prays for us in ways that cannot be put into words.

ROMANS 8:26 CEV

"And be sure of this: I am with you always, even to the end of the age."

MATTHEW 28:20 NLT

The dog who served as a model for Walt Disney's Tramp in *Lady and the Tramp*, was actually a lady. Disney bailed this female stray out of the city pound after she was spotted at the studio, then disappeared. She lived out her days at Disneyland.

Dodie Smith, author of the book that formed the basis for the Disney movie *101 Dalmatians*, named the canine hero after her first Dalmatian, Pongo. The scene where a puppy was revived shortly after birth came from an experience with a litter born to two of her Dalmatians.

Food for Wisdom

Lord, before I had a dog, I never thought
so much about what he should eat.
Now I often think about his treats, scraps,
and dog food. Help me feed my dog
wisely and well—but not too much.

If any of you lacks wisdom, you should ask God, who gives generously to all without finding fault, and it will be given to you. But when you ask, you must believe and not doubt, because the one who doubts is like a wave of the sea, blown and tossed by the wind. That person should not expect to receive anything from the Lord. Such a person is double-minded and unstable in all they do.

JAMES 1:5–8 NIV

So turn to God! Give up your sins, and you will be forgiven. Then that time will come when the Lord will give you fresh strength. He will send you Jesus, his chosen Messiah.

ACTS 3:19–20 CEV

A Pekingese is not a pet dog;
he is an undersized lion.

A. A. MILNE

Dachshund: A half-a-dog high
and a dog-and-a-half long.

HENRY LOUIS MENCKEN

There are all sorts of cute puppy dogs,
but it doesn't stop people from going
out and buying Dobermans.

ANGUS YOUNG

Having a hard time naming your new pup?
Go online and you'll find plenty of Web
sites that will help you out. You can choose
a name for your dog from any number of
languages, including Latin.

PAMELA McQUADE

Sometimes the heart sees
what is invisible to the eye.

H. JACKSON BROWN JR.

Homeless Pups

When I see an ad showing a hurting pup, my heart reaches out, Lord. I understand why some people end up taking in more animals than they can care for. But help me to be wise in caring, however many dogs I own.

*The LORD is a shelter for the oppressed,
a refuge in times of trouble. Those who
know your name trust in you, for you, O LORD,
do not abandon those who search for you.*

PSALM 9:9–10 NLT

*"For the mountains shall depart and the hills
be removed, but My kindness shall not depart
from you, nor shall My covenant of peace be
removed," says the LORD, who has mercy on you.*

ISAIAH 54:10 NKJV

*"I am leaving you with a gift—peace of mind and
heart. And the peace I give is a gift the world
cannot give. So don't be troubled or afraid."*

JOHN 14:27 NLT

Noticed it on a snowy day? The grown-ups
are all going about with long faces,
but look at the children—and the dogs?
They know what snow's made for.

C. S. LEWIS

No day is so bad it can't be fixed with a nap.

CARRIE SNOW

What is more agreeable than one's home?

MARCUS TULLIUS CICERO

"Let a sleeping dog lie." It is a poor old maxim, and nothing in it: anybody can do it, you don't have to employ a dog.

MARK TWAIN

Oh sleep,
It is a gentle thing,
Beloved from pole to pole.

SAMUEL TAYLOR COLERIDGE

Clearly, dogs believe every day should include at least one treat, whether it's a long walk in the park or a tasty bone. They know how to appreciate the simple but good things in life.

PAMELA MCQUADE

Search me [thoroughly], O God, and know my heart! Try me and know my thoughts! And see if there is any wicked or hurtful way in me, and lead me in the way everlasting.

PSALM 139:23–24 AMP

You are always making yourselves look good, but God sees what is in your heart. The things that most people think are important are worthless as far as God is concerned.

LUKE 16:15 CEV

The Lord bless you and watch, guard, and keep you; the Lord make His face to shine upon and enlighten you and be gracious (kind, merciful, and giving favor) to you; the Lord lift up His [approving] countenance upon you and give you peace (tranquility of heart and life continually).

NUMBERS 6:24–26 AMP

Why do dachshunds wear
their ears inside out?

P. G. WODEHOUSE

Bulldogs are adorable, with faces
like toads that have been sat on.

COLETTE

*Commit to the Lord whatever you do,
and he will establish your plans.*

PROVERBS 16:3 NIV

*Therefore confess your sins to each other
and pray for each other so that you may
be healed. The prayer of a righteous
person is powerful and effective.*

JAMES 5:16 NIV

From the lowly perspective of a
dog's eyes, everyone looks short.

Children left unattended will
be given a puppy or kitten.

Any member introducing a dog into the
Society's premises shall be liable to a fine
of one pound. Any animal leading a blind
person shall be deemed to be a cat.

Anybody who doesn't know what
soap tastes like never washed a dog.

About the Author

Donna K. Maltese is a freelance writer, editor, and writing coach. Mother of two grown children, she resides in Bucks County, Pennsylvania, with her husband. Donna is active in her local church and is the publicist for a local Mennonite project that works to feed the hungry here and abroad.